YO-BXW-200

seventeen presents...

500

style tips

What to Wear for School, Weekend, Parties & More!

HEARST BOOKS
A division of Sterling Publishing Co., Inc.

New York / London
www.sterlingpublishing.com

contents

school

weekend

party

date

work

pool

hey!

No more stressing in front of the **closet**, debating what to wear!
Consider *us* your personal **stylists**. This helpful book is jam-packed with cute outfit ideas and **quick** fashion tips—so you're sure to be the best **dressed** girl at *every* event.

–the editors of *seventeen*

school

Rocker or retro, sporty or preppy—no matter what your style, you want to feel pretty and look great. Use the ideas in this section for cute school-appropriate styles—so you can feel confident whether you're taking notes *or* sitting at lunch with your friends!

17 tip

Pick fitted—not-tight—pieces that make you look polished—not trashy—for class.

#1
wide-legged pants

do double duty: they add the look of curves to slim legs and thighs, and they balance a curvy tummy and hips.

great for all body types!

I ♥ Candie's 80'S

#2

Try a pair of tailored pants to dress up

a vintage-y tee.

#3
sparkly
jewels
**give any outfit a
touch of glam.**

#4
wear a belt

over a fitted jacket instead of through your belt loops for a cute, modern look. (The coin purse is an added bonus!)

#5

layer a track jacket
under your blazer for a unique look!

#6
wear a
woven
belt
**low on your hips
for a boho effect.**

#7

a bold-print tote

is a quick way to give your outfit some punch!

#8
a menswear
vest
**gets a softer look with a
fitted top and
a jeweled pendant.**

#9
a tailored blazer
instantly dresses up those edgy jeans.

great for
petite girls!

#10
a drop-waist
tunic
**is a trendy way to visually
elongate a short midsection.**

#11
super-
skinny
jeans
**look great under
longer tops so
you show off your
shape without
revealing too much.**

#12
flutter
sleeves

**bare your arms
in a subtle, school-
appropriate way.**

#13

a dress
**over wide-leg pants
streamlines hips.**

*great for
<u>curvy thighs</u>!*

#14

a button-down polo

**is great for layering over a
cami or under a sweater—or both!**

#15

pile on the bangles

to make any outfit a little bit funkier!

#16

Add personality to your book bag by safety-pinning on a

chain necklace.

#17

Give a layered tunic a more form-fitting shape with a low-slung belt.

great for an athletic figure!

#18
faded jeans that are lighter
in front and darker on the sides slim fuller legs.

#19
peep-toe
heels
**give your basic look
a fancier feel.**

#20
a trapeze
jacket
**looks as polished as
a blazer but
has a flirtier vibe.**

#21
double up skinny belts
over a dressy top for a funky edge.

#22

a guy's tie

works great as a cool belt.

#23

layer a turtleneck

under your favorite spring dress—and you can wear it throughout the winter, too!

#24
leggings
can make short shorts more appropriate for school.

#25

Pair a

vintage vest

**with a printed blouse;
the two quirky pieces will work
together perfectly.**

#26
boot-cut
cords
**are more polished
than jeans
but still look chic.**

#27

a shrug

keeps a bare dress from looking too risqué.

#28
wear flat shoes
with skinny jeans in the spring, then swap them for tall boots in the fall.

#29

a full skirt

is a classy way to girl-ify your sneakers.

#30
funky hair accessories
give *any* look an eclectic edge.

#31

a bold-colored trench

is the perfect pop of color for a gray, rainy day.

#32

Choose simple footwear– **nothing too chunky!—to wear with cropped pants.**

#33
capris

show off great calves (without being too clingy!).

great for curvy thighs!

#34
zebra print pieces
have a cool rocker feel—but only wear one at a time!

#35
be unexpected:
wear a studded belt with a delicate blouse.

#36

An oversize
metallic bag
**is big enough for
your books
yet trendy enough
for a party.**

#37

a big chain-link necklace

makes a plain henley look a little more glam.

#38
layer a
bright
tank

**under a striped
top for an
unexpected twist on
a nautical vibe.**

#39

Dress up an everyday T-shirt with vintage-y

rhinestones.

#40
a cropped jacket
is perfect for layering!

#41

drop pleats

look schoolgirl chic *and* don't add bulk to your middle.

great for <u>curvy</u> hips!

#42
mix a sporty jacket
**with more girly pieces
to get a flirty, unique style.**

#43
embroidery
on jeans adds a pretty touch to an otherwise plain piece.

#44
a little
ruching

**on your sleeves
subtly shows off
your arms.**

#45

wear furry boots

**with jeans and a cropped jacket
for a snow-bunny effect!**

#46

Dress up any pair of jeans by adding a
a belt with a
big buckle.

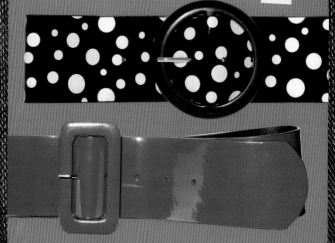

#47

Try an

argyle sweater

in candy-sweet colors for a modern preppy look.

#48

Wear a long-sleeve top under a slip dress **so you can wear it on cool days.**

#49
rugged
boots

add a cool edge to any girly outfit.

#50

Wear a frilly skirt to school with confidence— *a plaid top* **will dress it down just enough!**

#51

long jeans

make you look lean!

#52

Recycle your mom's old
vintage scarves
and use them as fabulous headbands!

#53

an A-line top

gives you curves in all the right places.

#54
a patent-
leather bag

**takes a basic blouse and
jeans up a notch.**

#55
a big buckle
and chains
gives any outfit a tough-girl touch.

#56

An oversize *hobo bag* **is a chic book-bag alternative.**

#57

show skin subtly—

**let a sheer top peek
out from under a cute jacket.**

#58

Make the
fedora
more wearable by
pairing it with
everyday basics, like a
sweater and jeans.

#59
capri lengths

solve the "they're not long enough!" problem—they're not supposed to be!

great for tall girls! →

#60
rhinestones
give a basic mini a little flash—
so you *really* stand out in
the hallways. But wear it with dark
tights when you're at school!

#61

girly
accessories
**can instantly dress up
any simple top and jeans.**

#62
a plaid pattern
creates the illusion of curves.

#63

layered tops

**look best when they have
different necklines and lengths!**

#64

Try cute

sneaker
flats

**to make a dress
casual enough for
school.**

#65

epaulets

have a trendy military look *and* visually broaden shoulders.

#66

Balance

a delicate
peasant
piece

**with an
unexpected, funky
touch of denim.**

#67
fun socks
make a pair of plain loafers cute and girly!

#68

pair a loose-fitting top

with sleek pants so you don't look shapeless.

#69
pin a
vintage-y
brooch
**in an unexpected
spot to make a plain
top special.**

#70

Put a polo shirt under a sweet V-neck **for a preppy vibe.**

#71

Glam up basic jeans by adding silvery or sparkly **accessories!**

#72

Pair a pretty
lace top
**with simple white jeans for
a feminine, vintage look.**

#73

tiny flowers
look boho chic on a soft skirt.

great for a <u>flat</u> butt!

#74
jeans with
**light shading on
the back and pocket details
help fill out your behind.**

#75
a baby-doll cami
enhances your bust and slims your middle.

great for petite girls!

#76
high-waisted pants
make your legs look longer.

#77

balance leopard print

with solid pieces or denim, and it's perfect for class!

great for
curvy thighs!

#78
bermuda
shorts
**with heels make your
legs look miles long!**

#79
slightly flared legs
look hot if you've got muscular thighs.

great for an athletic figure!

#80
a denim blazer
is versatile—you can dress it up or down.

#81
a fitted polo dress
is cute but still flirty.

#82
Tie on a
super-
long
sparkly
scarf
**to add glamour to
a classic polo.**

#83

long,
flared
bottoms
will lengthen legs.

*great for
petite girls!*

#84
try a high heel
with a floral detail—it's sultry, but sweet enough for school.

#85

Add cute patches **to your jeans to make them instantly unique.**

#86

a bright
pair of
boots

**and a belt give
just the right fun
touch to a
neutral trench.**

#87

**Shape a
flowy top by cinching
it with an**
embroidered
belt.

#88

a paisley-print top

**has a cool, boho vibe—
try it with a pair of cargo pants.**

#89
wear a bold top
with straight-leg jeans for rocker-chic style.

#90
add sparkly jewelry
to make a casual outfit look funkier.

#91

pair a hoodie

**with heels for the perfect
mix of sexy and sporty.**

#92

Play up the preppiness of a classic cable sweater with a denim mini and cute loafers.

#93

a blazer
**with structured shoulders
helps your upper
body look stronger.**

#94

Mix up your

floral patterns—

**try a bold bag with a
more subtle shirt.**

#95

a red skirt

can help you stand out in a sea of jeans.

#96

Printed
reversible
belts
**give you two looks
in one!**

#97

wear a wrap top
to make your waist look trimmer.

make your curves look great!

#98

girly
patterned
sneakers

**balance ripped
jeans with a touch of
femininity.**

#99

mix like-colored patterns

for a unique vibe—like graphic blue patterned tights with a delicate navy floral.

#100

Personalize your everyday book bag with

bright, fun
charms.

#101
a strapless top
can still be okay for school—wear a cute cardigan on top!

#102

Stick with
simple
tees
when wearing cool belts so the details really pop.

#103

When wearing
layered
tops,
**keep the necklines
similar—but not
identical—so you can
see both.**

#104

Collect

cute hats

**so you can save
a bad hair day!**

#105
long shorts
that hit just below midthigh are the right length for class.

#106

Layer a girly jacket over your concert tee **for an eclectic, vintage-y feel.**

#107

Wear a

fringed scarf

over a simple floral dress for the ultimate boho effect.

great for
a flat butt!

#108
flap pockets
add nice curves to your bottom.

#109

Pick a versatile

long necklace—

**it can be
worn full-length or
doubled up!**

#110
patent heels
look sophisticated with a pair of skinny jeans and a black sweater.

great for curvy hips and thighs!

#111

pants

with a smooth-fitting front and boot-cut legs are slimming.

#112

a studded belt
worn around your hips draws the eye to your cute butt!

#113

black jeans

are a sexy alternative to plain black pants.

#114

wear a
bangle

**high on your arm for an
unexpected yet
effortlessly cool look.**

#115
use a sequined sash
to dress up a basic pair of jeans.

great for girls with curves!

#116
A one-button blazer **defines your waist.**

#117

bright green
pops when you wear it with pale (or white!) jeans.

#118

pointy-toe flats

are always chic yet super-comfy.

weekend

Weekends are all about comfort and relaxation—but you can still rock your personal style, of course. Check out this chapter for casual, hangout-friendly outfits that'll make you feel super-cute—not sloppy!

17 tip

Adding pretty accessories to your lounging-around clothes instantly dresses them up!

#119

Give classic overalls a little sweetness with a *flowery top.*

#120

Mix a
casual jacket
**with a night-worthy belt—on
the weekend, anything goes.**

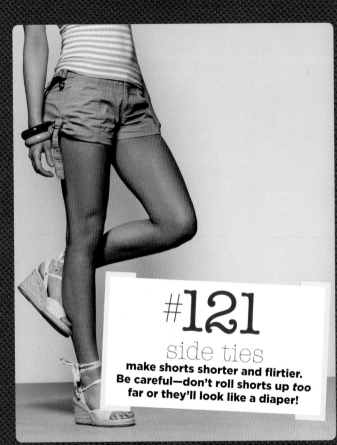

#121
side ties
make shorts shorter and flirtier. Be careful—don't roll shorts up *too* far or they'll look like a diaper!

great for an athletic figure!

#122

jeans

with a stretch fit are as comfortable as yoga pants and they glide over muscular legs.

#123

Pair a

track jacket

**with a mini for
the perfect weekend look.**

#124

Invest in a cute pair of

sunglasses—

they even look great as a headband!

great for petite girls!

#125
a short puffer
jacket adds volume to your figure.

#126

You'd think a
satin purse
**would be for dresses only, but it
goes great with edgy clothes, too!**

#127

A cute
designer bag
makes bargain outfits look expensive!

#128

When wearing a
tiny mini,
**don't bare too much
on top—layering is key.**

#129

a cute baseball hat

can be a lifesaver on the weekends— just throw one over a ponytail and go!

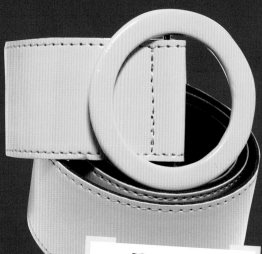

#130

Put on

a wide belt

**over a tee to cinch
your waist for a flattering
hourglass shape.**

#131

Wear a
bold
striped top
**instead of a solid
one—for an easy change
to your whole look.**

#132

fabric patches

give denim a boho vibe.

#133

Swap a trench coat's tie for a thick belt **to give your look a cool, eclectic feel.**

#134

layer your tops

**to add dimension while still
showing off your shape.**

#135

Pick a
sweatshirt
with graphics or
patterns that show off
your fun side.

#136

sneakers
**give a delicate
outfit an everyday,
wearable feel.**

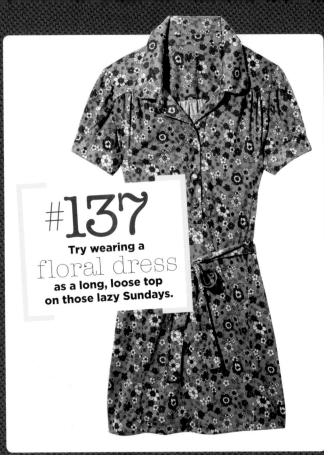

#137

Try wearing a

floral dress

as a long, loose top
on those lazy Sundays.

shows off the shape of your hips!

#138

For a funky edge, look for jeans with tough details like studding.

#139
pair pretty things,
like a cami, with more boyish basics, like long shorts.

#140

Create a new-wave '80s look by wearing just
one earring.

#141

Layer your
gym basics
for a hot look *outside* the gym.

shows off
a curvy butt!

#142
wear a rocker belt
with low-rise jeans to highlight your bottom.

#143

a slouchy tote bag

is made for the weekend—it holds everything and still looks cute.

#144
a funky hat
is the perfect way to hide that messy weekend hair!

#145

Pair a

rock tee

**with tough accessories
like a studded bracelet
or a cool wallet
chain for an edgy look.**

#146

wear retro knickers

with cute sneakers for a hip-hop vibe.

#147
go low!
Try a plunging neckline—you can work it without looking *too* exposed.

#148

Pair a
flowy top
**with tight pants
to create the right
proportion.**

#149
a bright cami

works like jewelry on the weekend— it adds a sparkle to any look.

#150

A dress can be as relaxed as jeans—just throw one on with a pair of fun sneakers.

#151

Unbutton the bottom of a
button-up dress
over jeans so it's comfier and even cuter.

#152
Wear a large
shoulder
bag
**diagonally across your
body to give it
a more casual feel.**

#153

Give a solid tee more of an earthgirl feel by throwing on an oversize

wooden necklace.

#154

a funky flat

is a comfy yet stylish alternative to sneakers.

#155

a hoodie
(half-zipped, of course!) makes a slinky, strappy top more casual.

#156

Wear

pearls

**with a sporty outfit to
add a feminine touch.**

#157

a Y-back tank

**shows off your back
in a flirty yet sporty way.**

#158
denim
in dark
washes
**always looks
rock 'n' roll!**

#159

try a
head scarf
**instead of a headband for
a little '60s flair.**

#160

a double-breasted
jacket adds curves to your shape.

#161

cargos

are great for hanging out: wear 'em loose, roll 'em up, and you're ready to go.

great for a pear shape!

#162

jeans with slanted pockets

make hips appear narrower.

#163

Give a classic

button-down

**a sexy edge by tying
it above your belly button.**

#164

**If you love
your long legs,**
short
shorts
**will let you put them
front and center.**

*great for
tall girls!*

#165
wedge boots

are more comfy than they look—the sole gives you height but doesn't hurt like heels can.

#166

Take multicolored
stripes
**to the next level—
wear a solid top that
matches one of the
stripes to make your
whole look pop.**

#167
a peasant
skirt
**and a slouchy bag
give you a boho look.**

#168

classic kicks
**look as cute with
jeans as they do with a mini!**

#169

a printed
thermal

**feels like pajamas
but look *so*
much more chic.**

#170
velour
gives sweatpants an old-school hip-hop vibe.

great for
an hourglass
shape!

#171

a snug-
fitting tee

**adds definition to
your upper body.**

#172

wooden
platforms

**have a casual look
but are comfy enough
for the mall.**

#173

Zip up a track jacket halfway to show off thick gold chains.

#174
loose-fitting
**jeans give a straight figure
a curvier look.**

great for *curvy hips!*

#175

Pants with
slant
pockets
in the front add
interest but don't
add bulk.

#176

a gray cropped hoodie

looks great with almost *any* color palette.

#177

A worn-in tee and a cropped leather jacket **were practically made for each other.**

#178

overalls
**are a comfy staple—try
some in a bright color!**

#179

a long top

**balances a pair of
super-short shorts.**

#180
stretchy low-rise
jeans flatter curves in a sexy way.

#181

Express yourself with
charms
that make a statement!

#182

a hoodie

tied around your waist makes a cute
belt *and* shows off your shape!

#183

turn a
dress into
a skirt
**by layering a tank
top over it!**

#184
pair slingbacks
in a pretty floral pattern with a sundress for an ultra-feminine yet comfy outfit.

#185

Find a tee that hits
below the
hips—
**it will look cute
peeking out from
under a hoodie.**

#186
embellished
sandals
**have a boho vibe—so keep
the rest of your
look simple and sweet!**

#187

argyle socks

and clogs look preppy in a playful (not geeky!) way.

#188
dark jeans
**are so versatile:
they can go from an
afternoon shopping to a
dinner out with ease!**

#189

Wrap a
scarf
**around your wrist
to make a
unique bracelet.**

#190
cozy booties
look cute with minis in the spring and fall. They'll still look good with jeans in the winter.

#191
Put a long cardigan over *short shorts* **to play down their length.**

#192
bleach spots
give denim an edgy feel.

#193

Mix a vintage-y tee with menswear-inspired pants and sneakers for a

cool-girl effect.

great for petite girls!

#194
midthigh-length
shorts elongate your figure by showing just the right amount of leg.

#195

**Cropped jeans
with cute details like**
cargo
pockets
**and button legs are
just right for lunch
with the girls.**

#196

a fun
necklace

**gives a relaxed
outfit a fun twist.**

#197

Rewhiten

sneaker soles

with whitewall car tire cleanser.

#198

a flowy
dress

**is a dream on a hot
day—the natural
movement of the
fabric keeps you cool.**

great
for a
full bust!

#199

wear two

contrasting tanks

to hide bra straps.

#200
rugged,
high boots
look hot with a miniskirt.

#201

detailing on
the pockets
of a mini fill out a small butt.

#202
cute printed
shoelaces
**will add a trendy touch
to your sneakers.**

#203

Layer long and short *chains* **to add playfulness to your look.**

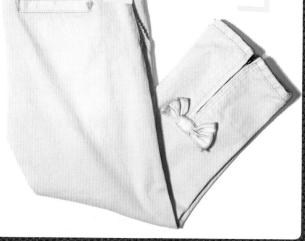

#204

Pants with a

feminine
detail
look fresh with printed sneakers.

#205
layer a bright hoodie
under a traditional blazer for a cool feel.

#206

Pair a denim mini with navy
sailor-striped wedges
for a classic preppy look.

#207

a romper
**in a soft cotton material
is as comfy as sweats!**

great for petite girls!

#208

Pants with a
hip-hugging
fit elongate a short torso.

#209

Just because you don't play soccer doesn't mean you can't make any outfit a bit more sporty with

soccer sneakers.

#210

**Transform your jeans—
cuff them to make instant**
capris!

#211

put a
cropped jacket
**over a white T-shirt
to spruce up a plain outfit.**

#212

Never throw away your
jeans—
**even when they're overly
worn, they still look cute.**

#213

**Finish your outfit in an unexpected way:
go for sneakers with bold laces or a**

funky design.

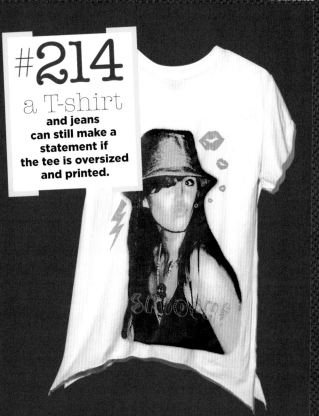

#214

a T-shirt

**and jeans
can still make a
statement if
the tee is oversized
and printed.**

#215

Add a splash of color to an understated all-white outfit by layering a bright yellow tank **underneath.**

#216

Dress up laid-back clothes with a shiny bag in a bold color.

#217

a jumper

adds a playful twist to your look!

#218

Slip on a pair of relaxed
*old-school
sneakers—*
**they add more personality
than gym sneakers.**

party

Round up your girls and hit the town...or even just your friend's house! Parties are the perfect opportunities to experiment with your style. This chapter is full of glam, eye-catching ideas.

17 tip

Put on just a *few* key accessories so you look trendy in a cute way—not like a cheesy fashion victim!

#219
slouchy
boots
**make any look cooler
and more casual.**

#220
gold or silver
sandals
**look totally hot with
a bold dress.**

great for prom!

great for petite girls!

#221

dresses

that are short and flouncy won't overpower a small frame.

#222

Put on brightly colored

plastic jewelry

**with going-out clothes
to give your outfit a sweet feel.**

#223

leopard accessories

are timeless—all you need is one little touch to make an impact!

great for prom!

#224

a wide satin waistband

fakes an hourglass shape.

great for prom!

#225

Try a dress with
semisheer
panels
**at the waist to reveal nice
abs in an understated way.**

#226

Tone down a fancy dress by pairing it with a sporty hoodie.

#227

Wear fitted black

pinstripe
pants

**with a fancy cami—
it's sexy to
mix masculine and
feminine looks!**

#228
kick pleats

show off long legs in a playful way.

great for __tall__ girls!

#229

a flutter-sleeved top
delicately frames strong arms.

great for an athletic figure!

great for prom!

#230

Wear a feminine dress with

sparkly accents

and you won't have to spend any money on jewelry!

#231

Choose a dress with a
high waist
to conceal
a curvy tummy.

great for
a curvy middle!

#232

When wearing a

low-cut top,

layer another tank underneath it so you don't show *too* much.

#233

When you wear high heels, bring jeweled or beaded flip flops **so you can switch your shoes if your feet start to hurt.**

great for prom!

#234
wear a skinny belt
**over a top to show off a
slim waist and curvy hips.**

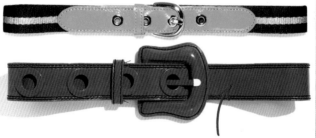

*great for
an hourglass
shape!*

#235

A big
jeweled
necklace
**takes any cute outfit
to the next level.**

#236

A dress with an

asymmetrical hem

reveals just a flash of leg: it's more elegant than a mini.

great for prom!

#237

pile on the bling!

Wear metallic hoops to accent a gold belt.

#238

Extra-long
pearl
necklaces
**can easily
double as belts.**

great for an <u>athletic</u> figure!

#239

a high neck halter top

accentuates shoulders in the most flattering way.

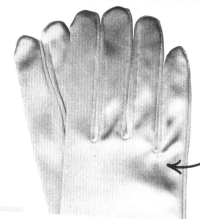

great for prom!

#240
remove gloves
at dinner, but wear them on the dance floor!

great for prom!

#241

Keep a

low-cut dress

**in place by securing
the fabric to your
skin with
double-sided tape.**

#242

**Wear a dress
without looking dressy—
pair it with**

flat sandals.

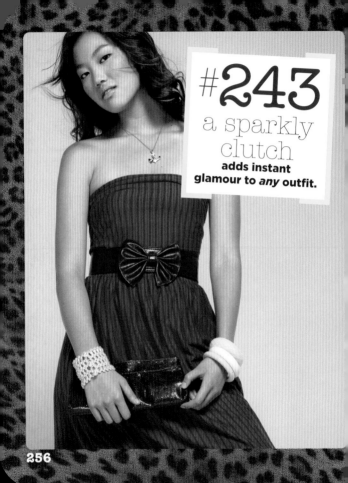

#243

a sparkly
clutch

**adds instant
glamour to *any* outfit.**

#244

Make a little black dress cuter by layering it

over jeans.

#245
super-high
heels
instantly elongate your legs.

great for petite girls!

#246

use bright
accessories
**to add color to a
neutral-toned outfit.**

#247

A contrasting
belt over
a jumper
gives extra shape to
your figure.

*great for
a straight body!*

#248

A fun string of
beads
**gives any look a little
personality.**

#249

oxfords

are good for school—but Oxfords with a heel are great for a night out!

#250
Use a
chain belt
**as a necklace—
no one will know you
improvised!**

#251

a chunky sweater

is a great option instead of a coat when you're going out at night.

#252

Accessorize with just a
pile of bangles
**and a men's watch for
the ultimate cool statement.**

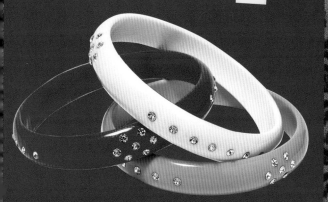

#253

Pick a
girly dress
**with lace trim.
It's sexy like lingerie—
but less revealing!**

#254
an edgy belt
can update an otherwise boring outfit.

#255

Fasten

ankle-strap shoes

***over* jeans for an eclectic touch.**

#256

Try a skirt with
ruffled
tiers
**or layered chiffon to
create curves.**

#257

Balance a tiny mini with a
boxy jacket—
it's fun to play with cool shapes.

#258
wear
western
boots
**under cuffed jeans
and a tank
for a modern style.**

#259

For a dress with heavy beading or detailing on the bodice, add a

sparkly bracelet

to draw the eye to the rest of your body, too!

great for prom!

#260

A floral dress in

satin

**is the quinessential
springtime party piece!**

#261

a metallic
shoe

**really stands out
when worn with
a chic black dress.**

#262
an extra-long pendant necklace
is a pretty centerpiece for any look.

great for
a **curvy** frame!

#263
an A-line dress
creates a sleek-looking silhouette.

#264
try wedges
**with chunky buckles
for an eclectic feel.**

#265

Layer a rocker
vest over a
minidress
**for an edgy
(yet classy!) look.**

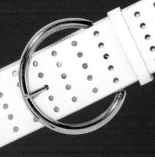

#266

Transform a simple dress by putting a low-slung
leather belt
over it.

#267

ivory satin

isn't just for weddings—it's a classic choice for prom that looks great on *any* skin tone.

great for a slim middle!

#268
put bangles
over your sleeve to give your
outfit a totally
sophisticated vibe.

#269

a little clutch

in a crazy bold color can work with almost *any* dress.

#270

double up

**your legwear—
colored tights under
fishnets look foxy
and keep you warm.**

#271

Wrap a few yards of sheer tulle **around your shoulders and secure with a sparkly pin over a formal dress.**

great for prom!

#272

Don't bring a

giant bag

**to a party! Make sure you carry a bag
that is *just* big enough for essentials!**

#273

A pair of
gold earrings
**gives any look just
the right amount of glitter.**

#274

a corset belt

worn over loose layers will give you a sexy shape.

great for a __full__ bust!

#275

When you wear

a halter dress

try a strapless or a halter bra so your straps don't show.

#276

Try a dress with a
bubble skirt—
**it adds curves
to straight figures.**

great for prom!

#277

a metallic bag

**is so versatile—
it goes with any dress color!**

#278

A ball gown with a
boned
corset
doesn't require a bra!

great for prom!

#279

**Wear accessories in the
same color
as your shoes to coordinate
your look in a playful way.**

great for prom!

#280

When attending a very formal event, choose a dress in

satin or silk—

the most elegant fabrics.

#281
bold purple boots

are a fun way to add an unexpected pop of color to your nighttime look.

#282

Try a mini with

footless tights

for a little more coverage.

#283
wear all black,
but keep it interesting: mix textures, fabrics, and patterns.

#284

A dress with a full, flouncy hem **makes hips look slimmer in contrast.**

great for curvy hips!

great for prom!

#285

Choose a dress with
rhinestones
and lace for a red carpet vibe.

#286

Put a multistrand

necklace

on—or mix at least three necklaces yourself.

great for <u>prom</u>!

#287

**Stand out
with a dress that has**
*feather
details—*
it's fun and flashy!

#288

Trade up your jeans from basic styles: sweet details **will make your look unique.**

#289
wear a big-buckle belt
to draw the eye to your hips.

great for
a **curvy** middle!

#290

an empire-waist

cut glides over your tummy.

#291
Add a touch of glitz with a
spangled bag.

#292

a boxy jacket

is the right proportion—and looks cute—with fitted long shorts.

#293

A shoe with a pointy toe and *high heel* **makes legs look long and lean.**

#294
a bold cap
can stand alone—no need to wear earrings or a necklace with it.

#295

black and
white stripes
make you stand out in *any* room.

#296

A skirt or dress with a

floaty
hem

**will make boyish legs
look curvier.**

*great for
a straight body!*

#297

pair
oversize
wedges

**in white crochet with
a sundress for
an easy spring look.**

#298

**Wear dark, slim jeans
with slightly**
flared legs—
**they fall
smoothly over high heels.**

#299

add long
beads
**to a textured tube
top—they'll lie flat
(and stand out).**

#300

Choose a pretty dress with

thick straps.

They'll act like a frame for amazing shoulders.

#301

Try a
drop-waist
tunic
**that skims your hips
to create
a great shape.**

#302
one big piece
of jewelry can make a stronger impact than a lot of little pieces.

#303

Try a bright,
wide belt
**low on your waist to
look curvier.**

#304

There's really only one occasion where you can wear

long gloves—

so take full advantage of the classic glamour of satin—from fingertips to elbow!

great for prom!

#305

low-slung,
skinny

**jeans always fit a straight
figure perfectly.**

#306
tiny polka dots
and a touch of lace have a sweet vibe that's so chic.

great for *prom*!

#307

adding a brooch

to your dress will draw attention to the nearest body part.

#308

Use a
set of pearls
to instantly dress up a
simple black dress—it's
so Audrey!

#309
cropped
leggings
**add edge to
a romantic dress.**

great for a small bust!

#310
A dress with a
gathered top
fills out your upper body.

great for a _full_ bust!

#311
a fitted, high-cut tank
minimizes your bust but still shows off your figure.

#312

To survive
high heels,
**stick padded adhesive
shoe cushions
inside your shoes.**

great for prom!

#313

a metallic bag

adds a little bit of party flash to a basic jeans-and-top outfit.

#314
asymmetrical ruffles
give a lacy gown an edgier feel.

great for prom!

#315

Pile on all your
favorite
accessories:
**if they're in the same
color palette, you won't look
overdone.**

great for a curvy frame!

#316

Dresses with an

empire waist

accent your bust and give you more room to move on the bottom.

great for prom!

#317

When you try a wild

cut-out shape,

**stick with classic (and classy) black
and white so your look stays chic.**

great for petite girls!

#318

If you want to add the illusion of height, try an outfit in

one solid color

to create a long, lean line.

#319

leave your lacy

bras in the drawer when getting dressed up: Styles with lace or ribbon will only create lumps and bumps under clingy tops!

#320

Wipe a dime-size amount of petroleum jelly on your patent-leather **shoes and rub in completely to give them a shiny, like-new finish.**

#321

A fun dress with a
big bow
**is a party staple—you're
like a pretty present all
wrapped up!**

#322

Style rules are looser for a party night—try

textured tights

under shorts for a change.

date

Whether it's a first date or a night out with your serious love, you want to look cute and confident—and just a bit flirty. Turn the page for sweet styles you (and he) will love.

17 tip

Sometimes one really interesting piece of clothing is all he'll need to remember you.

#323

earthy jewelry

is a way to show off your personality when you wear it with a simple top.

#324

a fitted
blazer

**draws the eye to
a tiny waistline.**

#325
peep-toe shoes
with pretty details like flowers and satin bows have a romantic vibe.

#326
lace details
**and flirty ribbons
make you look soft and
approachable.**

#327

Let a little

lace tank

**peek out from under your
jacket to look sweetly flirty.**

#328

When your skirt is super short, wear lots of layers on top **to balance your look.**

#329

a crazy piece of jewelry

shows your spontaneous, fun-loving side.

#330

Show off your
brightest shoes
by wearing capris!

#331

Girly details like

lace and satin
make basic jeans flirtier.

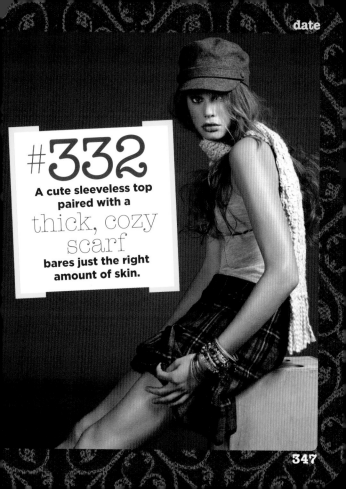

#332

A cute sleeveless top paired with a

thick, cozy scarf

bares just the right amount of skin.

great for a small bust!

#333

A lace-trimmed
V-neck dress
subtly fills out
a petite upper body.

#334

golden
accents

**give *every* look a
glam vibe.**

#335

an off-the-shoulder top
makes your upper body look broader (and your lower body look narrower)!

#336

layers

**are perfect for dates:
you'll never
get too cold in the
movie theater!**

#337

A-line skirts
look great on girls with curvy hips!

#338

dark leggings

**under a dress
create a sleek silhouette.**

#339

Wear a sexy
keyhole top
**for a cute way to show
just a tiny bit of cleavage.**

#340

Pick a pair of
tailored jeans
**long enough to
wear with heels for a
put-together look.**

great for a __small__ bust !

#341

a ruffle-trimmed

**cami fills out
a smaller chest.**

#342

Bring just a touch of

va-va-voom

to your favorite look with a glittery scarf.

#343

Look for a mini that has subtle
embellishments—
they'll definitely catch his eye!

#344
a strapless dress
**over jeans flaunts your
back in a subtle way.**

#345

a fitted coat

looks trendy *and* has a slimming effect.

#346
a handkerchief
hem
draws the eye to your sexy calves.

#347

halter necks

highlight a long neck and graceful arms.

#348

Give a basic tee a fancier look with a pretty

sweater shrug.

#349

When wearing an off-the-shoulder top, keep hair swept back and wear dangling earrings **to show off your neckline.**

#350
pair
feminine
wedges
**with a mini—they'll give
you height and up the
cute factor without
making you look trashy.**

#351

a slipdress

can be a great layering piece. Try it over a turtleneck and jeans or under a fitted blazer.

great for an hourglass shape!

#352
pick a
headband
**that contrasts with your
hair color so it pops!**

#353
a ribbon belt
draws tons of attention to your middle!

#354
lush-looking brocade
pieces will give you a romantic, Victorian look.

#355

Carry an

unusual bag

to give a classic outfit an unexpected, eclectic touch.

#356

A super-long
tunic
doubles as a
short flirty dress!

#357

Balance a

voluminous dress

by wearing a fitted tank underneath—it's a subtly sexy statement.

#358
a tie
sweater
**highlights a
small waistline.**

#359

Slim jeans and *wedges* **make legs look longer.**

great for
a <u>Curvy</u> frame!

#360
a soft fabric
**like jersey knit
skims over any bulges
and feels comfy!**

#361

To keep a chill off your shoulders without hiding your outfit, swap your coat or cardigan for a sweet shrug.

#362
a heart-print top
looks adorably retro *and* sends a subtle message!

#363

Wear a
charm necklace
to add a dash of color to a simple outfit.

#364
a skull-patterned
scarf screams coolness.

great for a small bust!

#365

A sweetheart neckline with
gathering
fills out your bust.

#366
a silky dress
layered under a sporty jacket combines a little flirtation with a lot of comfort.

#367

cuff your
jeans

**to show off just a
tiny bit of leg.**

#368
cute flats
with skinny jeans are perfect!

#369

Try a
glam dress
**with more casual pieces—
like flat sandals—
for a chic dinner look.**

#370

super skinny jeans

can work like tights— they show off your legs and look cool under dresses.

#371

For a feminine touch, wear a sequined cami **underneath a wrap cardigan.**

#372

a distressed
denim mini has a laid-back, "I'm low maintenance but still cute" vibe.

great for an athletic figure!

#373

an open-back top

is a dramatic way to show off a sculpted upper body.

#374

A dress with
an allover
print
plays up curves.

#375

**Instead of
matching your
shoes
to fit your outfit,
make them contrast
to show off
your great taste!**

#376

Try an oversize
cardigan
over a slip dress—it's
warm *and* boho-chic.

#377

dark
stockings
**and heels add a
sophisticated touch
to short shorts.**

#378

Wear a

strapless bra

**under a slinky camisole—
letting your straps show on a
date is tacky.**

#379

wear
stiletto
boots

**with tucked-in jeans
to show them off!**

#380

a boxy
jacket

**becomes super-sexy
with skinny pants.**

#381

**Give a flowing tunic
a sexier shape with a**

wide
leather
belt.

#382

High-heeled
ankle boots
**are a perfect
pair with skinny jeans.**

#383

Don't carry a

big bag

on a date—you'll look too
high-maintence.
Keep it small and chic!

#384

A tiny mini shows off your legs—but won't look *too* sexy when worn with cute

fuzzy
boots.

#385

colored hosiery

draws attention to your legs and makes them look shapelier.

#386

Use an
embellished
scarf
(instead of jewelry)
to give your black dress
lots of sparkle.

#387

slip on a loose shrug

to subtly cover your bust and play up your waist.

#388

Layered, chunky necklaces and *long, dramatic earrings* **draw the eye up to your gorgeous face.**

#389

an empire waist

skims over your curves and plays up your upper body.

great for a curvy middle!

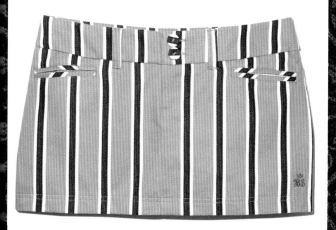

#390

a super-mini
works best with sneakers.

#391
a bright tank
underneath a sexy black-lace cami gives it a fun twist.

#392
animal prints

give off a sexy, spontaneous vibe.

#393

opaque tights
and rugged boots make a short skirt cool, not skanky.

#394
a shrunken cardigan
brings attention to your waist—yet it doesn't bare anything at all!

#395

a shift
dress
**flows right over your
curves but
looks super classy.**

*great for
a _curvy_ middle!*

#396

A structured

velvet
blazer
**is casual, rocker,
and polished all
at *once*!**

#397

Give light, relaxed layers a nautical feel by tying a rope belt **just above your waist.**

#398

Personalize a simple dress by pinning a vintage or

sparkly brooch

to the bustline—right where the straps meet the dress.

great for a straight body!

#399

a mini with soft pleats

gives boyish bodies a sexier look.

#400
a cute
dress

**in a pretty pattern
screams,
"Aren't I sweet?!"**

#401

To keep from showing too much skin, pair a hip-hugging miniskirt with a buttoned-up cardigan.

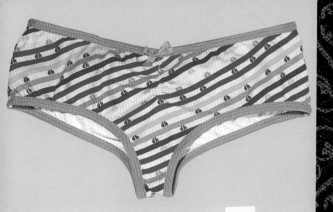

#402
hipster, boy-cut undies
**work great with low-cut jeans—
you won't show off your
butt whenever you sit down!**

#403
put a cami
**underneath a
tunic to create a flirty look.**

#404

A flowing skirt with a decorated waistband **highlights a small midsection.**

#405

Accessorize with
*a big
necklace:*
**it adds drama to a
simple dress!**

#406

Wear knee-high *flat boots* **to play up legs without adding height.**

great for tall girls!

#407
a knee-
length dress
makes legs look longer.

great for <u>petite</u> girls!

#408

Pair a black tee with a glittery
beaded shrug
for a sophisticated look.

#409

a wild floral design

paired with colorful shoes evokes the carefree '70s—it's a cool, fun statement.

#410

a bright tank

with a baby doll cut looks great with leggings.

great for an hourglass shape!

#411

a belted dress

shows off a tiny top half while hiding hips.

#412

Button a

sparkly cardigan

only at the top to show just a sliver of skin.

#413

Give a sweet dress a little edge with a studded bag.

#414

For a more casual date, a jumper is cute and incredibly cool.

work

Who says work clothes have to be stuffy?
Sophisticated and chic is key when you're getting
dressed for your internship or job, so don't be
afraid to add a unique touch or two to your buttoned-
up look. This section is packed with practical tips.

17 tip

Stick to tailored
looks that say you're
serious about work—
but try funky details
that show your
individuality.

#415

Step up basic
black and
white
with bright accessories.

#416
a proper plaid
**can still be fun in a fitted jacket
(but totally cool for work).**

#417

a floaty white sweater

is delicate *and* demure over a scoop-neck cotton top.

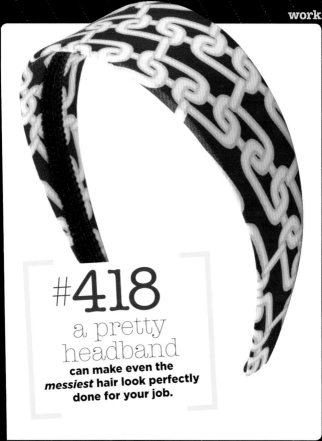

#418

a pretty
headband
**can make even the
messiest hair look perfectly
done for your job.**

#419

At a casual job,
you still need to
look polished with
simple
jewelry
and a neat belt.

#420
add a funky cardigan
to a dress to show off your cool side.

#421

**Cinch a loose-fitting
dress with a**
ribbon
for a cool, retro feel.

#422
tuck khakis
into high boots for a look that's trendy but still neat.

#423

blazers

always look professional—layer a soft blouse under one for a more feminine take.

#424
flared trousers
look sophisticated *and* don't cling to your curves.

great for <u>curvy</u> hips and thighs!

great for a *straight* body!

#425
wide-leg pants
make your body look curvier and they're always work-appropriate.

442

#426

Try a wide,
waist-cinching belt
over **your blazer for
a trendy take
on a classic piece.**

#427

Pair a

shruken jacket

with a long tunic top to look sophisticated— but still hot!

#428

Balance conservative

pinstripes

with a frilly brooch.

#429

an oversize
string of beads

**adds a fun pop to a
conservative work outfit.**

#430
One bold piece like
wide-striped
pants
**is all you need to stand
out at the job.**

*great for
curvy thighs!*

#431

Always keep a
soft sweater
around. It gets chilly in the office!

#432
a cropped blazer
lets you show off a cool belt.

#433
a floral necklace
**adds instant girliness to
any basic work look.**

#434
a black pencil skirt
is a timeless staple that always looks polished.

#435

Be a little cheeky by wearing

your little
brother's tie.

#436
try cropped pants
in a menswear-inspired plaid. (high heels make you look girlier!)

great for petite girls!

#437

Balance a
bold print
**jacket by wearing it
with a pair of jeans and
a solid top.**

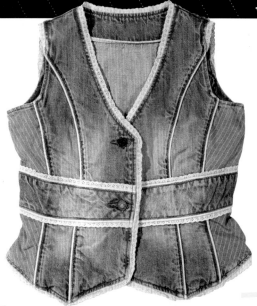

#438
dress up a denim vest
with a sweet skirt and work-appropriate flats.

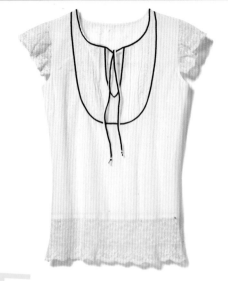

#439

a soft blouse
looks professional with a simple skirt.

#440
fitted
capris
**worn with high
heels give you a sleek
yet feminine vibe.**

#441

For work, make sure a

button-down shirt

doesn't gap open over your bust!

#442

Style a
metallic
braided belt
**over a flowing floral dress
to play down its sweetness.**

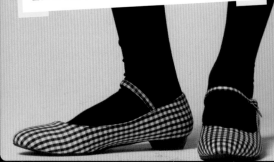

#443

Give your outfit a preppy twist with
houndstooth flats.

#444

a fun pendant

lets your personality shine through your work outfit.

#445

a swingy floral dress

is ideal for work—it looks soft and pretty but feels unbelievably comfy.

#446
add dangling earrings
to highlight a beaded trim or a special embellishment.

#447

To brighten a simple look, tie a

scarf or ribbon

into a loose, exaggerated bow around your waist.

#448
Layer a
turtleneck
**under a dress—and you can
leave your cardigan at home!**

#449

Wear a

fitted jacket

**buttoned up as a top—it's a fresh
way to look pulled-together.**

#450

**Add a little drama to
your outfit: wrap
a bead necklace around
your wrist as a**
bold
bracelet.

#451
pinstripes
go great with strong, brightly colored accessories!

#452
a knee-length skirt
balances super-long legs.

great for tall girls!

#453

Dress up a pair of cargos **with a lacy cami and high-heeled wedges.**

#454

a denim
pencil
skirt

**is nice enough for
work yet cool enough
for school.**

#455

a cute
brooch
**adds interest to a
plain work tote.**

#456
a collared shirt
doesn't have to feel stuffy—when trimmed with lace, it's girly and sweet!

#457

Try pearls with a
hint of color
**(like pink)—it's a modern take on
an age-old classic.**

#458

open-toe shoes

can be a job staple if you pair them with dark tights.

#459

Pin a classic *cameo* **to your jacket as a unique, vintage-y accent.**

#460
try one solid color
to streamline your hips and bust.

great for an hourglass shape! →

great for petite girls!

#461

a to-the-knee pleated skirt

creates a lean line, so your body looks taller.

#462

A necklace with chunky, dramatic links **makes a casual outfit look bold.**

#463

flowing,
wide-leg
pants
**look best with a
fitted top.**

#464

a full skirt

**that hits close to the
knee draws the
eye to your calves.**

great for a curvy frame!

#465

Make a revealing

wrap-around dress

okay for your job—put a tee under it and a fitted blazer *over* it.

#466

The longer your

pants,

the longer your legs look (but don't let them drag on the floor—that makes you look shorter!).

#467

For the most comfort, buy

pointy-toe
shoes

**a half size bigger than usual.
This way, your
toes won't feel crammed in.**

#468

A bold
pattern
dress
***can* work at your job—just tone it down with a solid cardigan.**

#469

mix and match

a cute blazer with pants–it's professional but has more personality than a stuffy suit.

#470

When wearing high heels **at work, pair them with long trousers (never a short skirt!) so you look professional.**

#471

a funky,
patterned
scarf

**adds a little personality
to your work clothes.**

#472
a pop of blue
will amp up any conservative outfit.

#473
a boxy blazer
has super-chic '60s flair.

#474

glen plaid

is so subtle, it's barely a print—you can pair it with almost anything, like a bold sweater.

pool

It's hard for anyone to turn down **poolside** fun or a day at the **beach** with friends. Make the most of it by looking *hot* in your swim gear! Check out this chapter for the styles and fits that **suit** you best.

17 tip

Wearing the right suit for your body type will help you feel confident—so you'll have more fun!

#475

a red
swimsuit—
**in *any* style—
instantly grabs attention.**

#476
a bandeau top
means no weird tan lines.

#477

a straw bag

with leather trim is casual enough for the beach but pretty enough for going out.

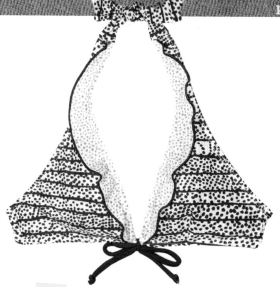

#478

a tie-front top
creates subtle cleavage.

#479
a cutout
swimsuit
is a flirty way to show a lot of skin without wearing a bikini.

#480
underwire
creates shaping and coverage that feels like your favorite bra.

#481
string bottoms
actually have a narrowing effect on your butt—seriously!

great for a curvy butt!

billabong

#482

a tube dress
**is easy to slip over a bikini
and to roll into your bag.**

#483

a high-cut suit

makes legs look longer.

great for petite girls!

#484
boy-cut
shorts
**create the illusion of
curvier hips.**

*great for
a straight
figure!*

#485

a high-cut string bottom

works on everyone's hips— it's completely adjustable!

#486
oversize
sunglasses

create instant glam.

#487

a one-piece

can be cute and sexy (and not the least bit swim team-ish)—just look for a bright color and a low neckline.

#488
Tie your
string bikini bottoms
high on your hip—it will visually lengthen your legs (instead of cutting them off in an unflattering way).

#489

a graphic pair
of shorts

look fun with a solid bathing suit.

#490
horizontal
stripes
**fill you out and give the
look of curves.**

#491
A ruffled
skirtini
**adds some volume to
your backside.**

great for a small butt!

#492

a tankini

is slimming and is just as sexy as a bikini.

#493

Layer a
*striped
bikini top*
**under your solid
shirt to go from beach
to street.**

#494
a swim skirt
makes every body look narrower.

#495
a wild
pattern
**makes your body
look hot—and
puts all eyes on you!**

great for a full bust!

#496

halter tops

**offer the best support
while giving
you a flattering shape.**

great for a
small bust!

#497
an embellished
**top fills out your
chest in a subtle way.**

#498

aviator
sunglasses

**have a timeless style and give
off a cool retro vibe.**

#499

Create a cute
waistband
**by letting your swimsuit
bottoms peek out
from underneath jeans.**

#500

A pull-on cotton
minidress
**slips over any swimsuit
when it gets cloudy!**

index

u

v

photos